#25856
7.50

Out of Silence into Being

AF810991

Out of Silence into Being

Selected Poems

by Rebecca Camhi Fromer

REGENT PRESS
Oakland, California

Copyright © 2007 by Rebecca Camhi Fromer
All rights reserved.

ISBN 13: 978-1-58790-127-0
ISBN 10: 1-58790-127-7
LCCN: 2006937897

Etchings by Abram Krol
Lithograph by Pinchas Litvinovsky

PRINTED IN THE U.S.A.
Regent Press
6020-A Adeline
Oakland, CA 94608
www.regentpress.net

You do not need to leave your room. Remain sitting at your table and listen. Do not even listen, simply wait. Do not even wait, be quite still and solitary. The world will freely offer itself to you to be unmasked; it has no choice. It will roll in ecstasy at your feet.

— Franz Kafka

Table of Contents

Author's Note

Someone or something, perhaps a circumstance of long duration, chance sight or flight no greater than a moment, a random thought begging fruition, or a gnawing desire to enter into the jaws of a mystery, inspires the poet to seek the adventure into and beyond the fleeting time, arresting it, as it were, in an effort to express that which in essence is not ordinarily seen, heard, known or thought of in the world of daily preoccupation, or has been said differently by thinkers throughout time. The excitement of discovery, sometimes to his own surprise and delight, not only makes all labor seem worthwhile, but also explains why without that greatest of rewards, the poem would not exist; literature, music and art would not exist, beauty and insight would hide their color and light, the world could not be understood, and life would be unbearable without the dance of an idea, sound, provocative thought, or particular vision of the universe.

— Rebecca Camhi Fromer
Berkeley, California

Preface

There is nothing like my mother's writing. Nothing like her literary sensibilities. Nothing like her use of words, her love of words, her word combinations, and her precision. She is a master of precision.

Perhaps one of the most important things she taught me, and that I in turn hope I've taught my children, is the power invested in the turn of a phrase. For my mother, every word has a sense of purpose. This almost animistic quality of language has captured my imagination as, most likely it has captured, or will capture yours. The words don't just flow, they captivate.

What I wished most to see in this volume was, well, everything. My critique is that there's not nearly enough in here to get a full sense of the power of my mother's use of language, the power of her imagination, and the complexity of her ideation. What I wished was that all of her written works were collected here; all of her poetry, all of her plays—in full rather than in excerpt—as well as her essays, and even her treatise on I.B. Singer, which remains one of my favorites.

What I wish now (since my original wish was so clearly unreasonable) is that you could hear these works aloud, see them performed, hear my mother's tales on their inception, their construction. What I know now, is not only that you will enjoy these two volumes immensely, but also that my mother's voice is indeed resident within the written word.

In the above, I have given you a brief introduction into the mind of a remarkable woman who has captured many lifetimes in the cadence of her song. What you will find is sometimes mournful, sometimes joyous, sometimes wry and always, always a work of intellect tempered by the folkloric legacy of her Sephardic soul.

Mira F. Z. Amiras, PhD
Professor, Comparative Religious Studies,
Coordinator, Middle East Studies SJSU

Part One

For Daniel Pearl

The cobra hears the overture;
He hears the strains, and writhes
Sinuously to such innocence;
He is tense; he is attentive,
Ready to lure; ready to strike,
For the man who speaks is young,
And ripe for a day's amusement.
The jolly day has already begun,
But a foreigner may be forgiven
For trusting in honor among men;
He has journeyed far; he is eager
To hear what the cobra has to say;
It is why he has entered its nest;
It is why he is alone and unarmed,
Artless mind in place, pen and pad
In hand; let me hear your story,
He says. Will you help me, he asks,
And the seducer replies with wile:
Tomorrow, at the café. Be here.
Thus, in two words the clock is set,
The sheath cast off,
The seeds of deception sown.
There is an excitement astir now,
And the young man's heart quickens;
He wants to meet; he must understand,
And he means to get at the truth here.
The night sleeps; the dawn wakes,
But he paces, dreaming of his violin,
The bed too large, with none to share it.
He will have other dreams soon enough,
And dread nightmares by the score.
The cobra will strike, the boa will constrict,
Truth will pinion and engulf him.
The fury of a dark age awaits us,
The clouds are above, it has begun.

The Scholar

The man has a kindly face,
Almond eyes soft as down,
And a poetic cadence
To each sound he utters
In conveying thoughts.
His words take wing;
He speaks with joy,
And nuances soar
Into song, for he sings;
He caresses and lifts words;
He tosses them as in play,
And so doing, conjures worlds,
Journeying into them as one
Unsealing the lid of time.
With spellbinding evocation
Inseparable from events,
He casts nets, pitches tents,
Thirsts across hot, dry sands,
Trades along caravan routes,
Fends off brigands, and writes
Of loves and longing and loss,
Each word a pearl, every thought
A jeweled necklace, the strands
Of which tell our tales through time,
For history is the clay of his being,
And language the love of his life.

We are seized with thirst and
A hunger not new, but absent
For longer than we realized;
We have felt the ebb and swell
Of passions ruling destiny,
And sense what he does not say—
What he would not say so nakedly.
In rhythms obedient
To his heart, he has touched ours.

Imagine! See! Understand! Read!
Do you not hear the beat of it?

The Second Meeting with the Scholar

He is infatuated, and more;
He is in love with the poets;
He cannot help himself.
He is intoxicated, the air
He breathes, rarified;
He wafts above the world,
Aloft on their words,
Whirls with currents
Above the panoramic fray,
Touches the skies, and
Dazzled by the lapis night,
Reaches for the stars.
Look here, the poets say;
There is yet more of wonder.
And *lo!* He plummets
Into the frothing sea,
He plummets into the
Blue-black cold swirl of
Silence in wondrous depths,
And he swims as never before
Among marvels and portents
In the fluid night, his mind
A luminous conveyor
Of the shimmering light
That lies fathoms deep in sea.
Look here, the philosophers say,
There is yet more of wonder.
And *lo!* his feet sink
Into the sands of old shores
And new. You have scaled heavens
That hold distant futures in store;
You have plunged into wide seas

And probed the embryonic past,
But dear fellow, here you stand,
And here you shall remain a day.
Now we begin: thus do they speak.
It is time, they say. Come along,
They beckon. They tease and
Tweak his ear, whet his appetite,
Thump his forehead but once,
And dazzle him with the force
Of reason and the dance of mind
That so arouses his senses. First,
Savoring chaos and calamity,
Reversals of order and fate,
They hold him fast, lest he faint,
And then, enrapt in awe,
The revelations of how to live,
What to do, and how to die
Unravel in great simplicity.

The Third Meeting with the Scholar

Era bueno de une rey . . .
Once upon a time, there was a king . . .

Conta las cantigas de tiempos pasados,
Sing the songs of times past
Quando estuvimos en tierras ajenas,
When we were in strange lands
Y aprovimos bivir di dia en dia
And tried to live from day to day
Con il fuego enfrente de los ojos
Confronted by the stake in sight
Y il mabul a la puerta.
And the deluge at the door.

The lion roars, the lamb lies in wait;
He is not fleet; he bides the tides.

The butcher, a shadow at his heels,
Readies the knife; readies the appetite,
Athirst, like a dormant dog aroused
By the scent of blood, bone and flesh
Of the virginal, sweet and tender kid.
Ay, yay, yay, la vida es une sueno.

Demons breach the cavernous dark,
And angels hide their countenance;
Kings of city-states, kind or cruel,
Fickle or true, mortals all subject
To fate, ride the crest of power and
Its resounding, thunderous decline,
All the while testing human endurance
Upon the fiendish cross of infinite pain
Embedded within the blood-rich loam
Of broad latitudes and vast reaches.

The inscrutable voice of god
Beseeched by all, denied to all
And heard by none but the mad,
Who dare to wear the mantle
Of those anointed in dreams
Laden with signs and wonders,
Now bring joy, brief respite,
And confounding despair
When delusion unseals its blind eye
In the scorching light of day.

Recantation or triumph of spirit
Now fills the theater of life
In the days of raging plagues,
Dark ages, and luminous minds,
Both silenced and outspoken,
And behold, an elliptical language
Erupts; it blooms like wildflowers
In a field of rainbow-filled dreams,
Its roots in imagination, and its thirst

Quenched in beds of desire to the glory
Of intimacy and abomination alike,
In candor and in secrecy and by design,
For the righteous have been subdued
And the straightforward have been crushed,
Plundered, dispersed, and ravaged,
Pitched from precipitous cliffs,
Or cast into chasms and frothing seas.

Yes, all this and diabolic invention
Awaited believer or heretic alike,
So why not an order of opposites?
Why not secret teachings, secret
Rites, secret meetings, and secrets
Within secrets for the appointed one?
The worthy of worthies? the fledgling,
Into the mysteries of mysteries?
Alas, my dears, the hour is late.
I'll take your questions now.
Any questions? You, in the back.
Yes. *You! Over there! Speak up.*

The Fourth Meeting with the Scholar

A wanton wind keens across
Vast stretches of verdant land,
Its eerie empathy to events
Surreal to the attentive ear.
Burdened clouds veil the sun,
And spill their cache of rancor
Amid the cobblestone byways
Of the *Juderia,*
And the slaughters begin,
The conversions begin,
The appropriations begin,
The disputations
And dislocations begin.

Perhaps nature knows how to mourn
Man's misalliance with the stars,
Or perhaps we have come from fire
And forgotten the sea within.
Are we not all matter, and both?
Thunder rolls, cracks and roars;
Lightning slashes the night sky
With ear-splitting urgency;
The rainbow absents itself
From the morning sun
After the fall of fresh rains,
And the orange blossom holds
Its breath, its essence confounded
In the wake of a persistent stench.

For a century, the storm brews,
Garnering strength for great days,
Or days destined for greatness
In a unified, intolerant nation,
Wrought about by foul means
Called fair, with justification
In the name of God Almighty.
But oh, what virtue have we here,
When the frenzy, if not fervor
To convert the Jew, has one eye
On avarice and empty coffers
Of Holy Office and state,
And the other, on an obsession
Laced in an infamous sadism
Of those who, by their acts,
Diminished what they professed?
Were all meek and compliant? No.
Were all silent and impotent? No.
Was there unity of outlook? No.
Were reasonable men to be coerced
Or convinced? Sometimes, yes.
Were rabbis among them? Yes.
Were poets and scribes? Yes.

Were women consigned to flame? Yes.
And young men, too? Yes.
Were any burned in effigy? Yes.
Were estates confiscated? Yes.
Were New Christians skeptical? Yes.
Were New Christians believers? Yes.
Were the poor harassed? Not at all.
Did they have lands? No. Monies? No.
Was ritual murder attributed to the Jew?
Was poisoning of wells attributed to the Jew?
Was the incidence of the Black Death,
Or sorcery, perhaps? What do you think?
Did the debacle end in expulsion? Oh yes.
Was it successful? It depends on outlook.
Did the miseries of 1391-1492 end?
Are you dreaming? Well then,
Were these noble practices spread
By Spain into the New World?
Oh yes. And elsewhere? Oh yes.

The Spinning Wheel

First Addendum to Fourth Lecture

We leap through time and space.
The currents are swift; the swells
Are overwhelming, and the tides brush
The contours of consciousness.
New thoughts about life and death
Sprout in the soils of the soul
To embrace a young man's torment,
A spirit rent for a mother's grief.
On the morrow he lives no more,
His life forfeit to false premises,
Hysteria, virulent as the plague,
And a needless death,

A death steeped in irony,
But who dies as he, so loftily
Triumphant in the last hours,
A poet's ordered meter writ plain
On paper his pen will see no more,
His lips meant for lingering kisses
In the throes of love, and silenced
But for us who read his lament?

The Spinning Wheel

Second Addendum to Fourth Lecture

What does one say to one
Who opens wide the door
To the shafts he has mined,
To the rich deposits he has
Discovered and excavated?
To the raw materials refined,
And to all treasures shared?
What does one say to one
Who has known the dark cavern
As a slave, and has risen like
Lazarus, whole and free to
Reenter the pit and breathe life
Into the shards of clay found there?
What does one say to one
Who all but shouts: look about:
History is not dead; make it;
Illuminate it; lift its sparks
To join the star-filled lapis night?

The Fifth Meeting with the Scholar

All does not go well.
The dense forest obscures the light,
Thickets and bramble obtrude the way.
A prickly corridor awaits the traveler
Seeking the open sky and fields
With no compass in hand.
Seeds of random thoughts scatter
Across the stretches with promise
Until, at last, purpose unfolds
Its glorious petals.

It has to do with thinking,
It has to do with language,
It has to do with meaning!
We cannot be stupid about it.
It has to do with usage—
Words to expunge and never utter
Again without searing consciousness.

It has to do with the prestige,
Perhaps rightly denied the rapacious,
Hungry ghost seeking a seat of honor
At the tables of the great and learned,
And it has to do with prestige
Granted, or prestige protracted
Far too long for mortal man to bear.

The Sixth Meeting with the Scholar

A surge of energy bursts forth.
We chat in clusters, sensuously
Savoring pistachio halvah
Between obliging fingertips
Readied lips, and coffee cups in hand.
Delicious: it is simply delicious to cohere

As one, and to feel how well we knit
Into a seamless, inspired whole.
Atop a high, strong limb
Warmly and safely-ensconced
In cocoon-like intelligence,
The metamorphosis' mystery
Retains its secret in silence
Within a wondrous dark cloister,
Where wings and a glory of color
Await the marvels of waking
To herald transformation at dawn,
And a momentous fragility.

We are astir, a contagion of interest
Alive in our eyes and in the intensity
Of curiosity that fills the room.
Who is this man? What does he write?
Where does he come from,
And who among us is brave enough to ask?
What does he teach? Where is he going?
The appetites have been whet;
The time is short, the man is important;
For now, he is here, but we already miss
The many tomorrows without him.

We soar in the expanse of imagination
On his unerring outstretched wings,
And the descent into past times is effortless.
It dissolves the present, which has made way
For an event of manifest grace
In the safety of the eager, open mind.
We are now among the poets of intrigue;
Poets who slander and betray and heap
Calumny upon their fellows,
Sycophants who preen and scrape,
In cowardly retreat from essence,
Ingratiatingly heedless of harm,
As envy, intrigue, and presumed favor
Override conscience.

The silent ones do their work in secret.
They are the scribes, and they report
On history; they comment on it unabashedly,
Passionately opposed to tyrannies old and new.
They have something to say about morality;
They have something to contribute to conscience;
They are the voice of what little humanity remains,
And they keep the candle burning against the dark cave
Or veiled faces of deceitful men—to whom ambition
Is a sport or drive to vanquish another,
And who construe power as domination,
Little knowing true strength best lies
In conquest over the self.

The Seventh Meeting with the Scholar

I was to give the main address,
But they didn't let me speak
And I asked myself why I was there.
Why had I traveled so far?
You let me speak; you ask questions.
I like that. I like coming here.
We have a lot to cover, and I want to finish.
Next week, we will have questions,
Only questions. I'll answer them all.
Think about them; write them down.
I don't want to talk about my trip.
In any case, it was dreadful.
Too many introductory remarks,
All of them pedantic twaddle
And posturing. No one understood
Anything. Not a word! *And what accents*!
You and I understand one another.
I can talk to you; you can talk to me.

The language has no future,
And universities can't teach
What they don't know of the past.
Who can comprehend so vast a calamity
As life affords, ages construe, and tyrants rewrite?
But this lady speaks Ladino;
She knows it. Listen to her.
She is among the last, the few.
Start there, but as for the conference?
It was no conference at all.
Someone whispered in my ear:
"Can you translate?" I said yes,
Like a fool, and hours into the long night,
The self-adulation I now confronted
Whirled me into the vortex of a vanity
I could not fathom and longed to escape.
One suffers invisible chains,
And I yearned to break free and breathe.

My talk should have begun an hour ago,
And I should be concluding my remarks.

Speaker after speaker droned on heedlessly,
And I deciphered it all until, at last,
None other than I remained.
"Can you make it short?" I was asked.
Short? How short? **"Short."**
Five minutes? Six minutes? How short?
"Five minutes." *Okay. I'll make it six.*
That night I ached to be back home,
But by morning, my spirit returned.
The worst is over. We are a potpourri
Of hothouse flowers and rare specimens,
And what is so remarkable about that?
The strangeness I feel will pass,
I thought, as I braced myself,
But the newborn day was not meant
For reaping the brave seeds of hope.

I have been away too long, traveled too far,
Forgotten too much or grown too old,
And I was quite wrong to assume anything.
We had not managed to deconstruct
The towering obstacles to meaning
That hid one thought from another,
When sudden panic gripped the room,
And those I supposed to be both phlegmatic
And bloodless, shot up and scattered with a cry.
Tella novella, tella novella, they whooped,
And the room emptied; everything shut down.
My god, I wondered. What have I missed? When?
Where have I been, and what is tella novella?
Only slowly and to my sad regret,
I learned soap opera is understood by all,
And that television will survive
Without translation,
To enter the fiction of our lives

The Eighth Meeting with the Scholar

You have asked a vast question
Of importance to many,
And touches upon my views,
But I am not a prophet,
Nor do I pretend to be.
If you want my opinion
On the matter, I will speak.
You may not agree with me,
But I will address the truth
As lived upon my own flesh,
For my blood has paid the price
To speak with authority—
To formulate a judgment
Based upon experience—
And it has spilled its substance
On a thirsty, arid land

Now topical in the news
In dire need of direction
Worthy of two great peoples
Grown weary of attrition,
Who yet cling to sinful pride
And unyielding warriors.

I fought and bled for this land
When I, a youth, wished to live
The life of manly vigor
In better arms than I then held.
I led men into battle,
Good men all, who bleed as I
Or die of inflicted wounds
On both sides, and not just ours.
I served in many campaigns
And not once could I claim love
For the brutal commander
I know so well and abhor.

I lived, I learned, and I built.
I tilled my best soil, my mind.
The breath of art and beauty
Daily restores me anew
With hope for mankind's genius.
I do more than scrutinize
Scraps in dusty libraries,
But I say to you, my friends,
The contested land we love
Is not without a blemish.
Our course is not always just;
We have rabid elements,
A megalomania
Inherited from this shore;
A stubborn, wild man or two
From our own and other shores,
Who destroy in a rampage,
Scorn rights contemptuously,

And humiliate good men,
To whom just regard is due.
We both have claims to honor;
Let us do so with dispatch.

Tikkun

Son of Islam,
Cultivator of grace,
Delicacy of detail,
Grandeur of mind,
And generations
Of toleration,
Mentor, long friend
And compatriot of the Jew,
Master of mathematics,
Scanner of the skies,
Doctor of sciences,
Healer, builder, thinker,
Teacher and poet;
Great warrior,
Strong in wisdom,
Who once walked
In soft shoes,
Wore robes of silk
And belts of silver,
And whose rapt head
Engaged in learning
And paid homage to faith,
Let your women be free;
They are virtuous.
Let your children learn;
They are worthy;
Let academies and libraries
Rise out of the blight of neglect,
And let them attain the heights
Of the architectural dream.
We will meet you there,
By the lavish, blue tile fountain,
And walk under the lofty arcade
In the heat of a troubled day.

Part Two

A writer thinks
Of his subject.
It is a phantom,
An elusive,
Disembodied essence
That seeks form
In the mastery
And mystery of a word;
It is a climb
Upon the rungs
Of an invisible stair,
A fever,
A rage
He is possessed by,
An attack,
A grip, a hold,
A madness,
An act, a curse,
And wisdom dreams
That salvage the soul.

It is a vision,
A finding,
A discovery,
A gift
And completion
Without end,
A breath
Of the pulsating universe,
Existence beyond time
Bred within the bosom
Of placental vapors,
A burst of mind stars
Creating new worlds,
And a wonder
Firing the imagination
With the pearl
Of long irritation,
But, and not to mislead,
The last word must be
That it is a discipline.

Kaleidoscope

Weakness of will
And thrust of brute flesh
Or self-righteousness
In defense of casual war,
Deaden the soul,
And it is the first victim.

I.

Men wage war, slay and slash,
And, good patriots all,
Will pillage as victors,
Rape freely, as by right,
Or in the wake of day
And lucid afterthought,
Rage at the misdeed
And its sad aftermath,
Ashamed, perhaps, to see
That beneath the self's sheath
Lies another dark soul,
Which is also himself.
A man enters a war
Innocently enough
Before his eyes open,
But alas, worlds will die
At his hands and with his arms,
And none can erase that stain.

II.

A combat field breeds
The limbs of former men;
A sorry crop, a sad sight
Of strewn viscera
Hosts an army of insects.
Repentance does not avail.
The bed of love is empty,
The beloved is gone,
And we call him a hero.
One day, the clod will do,
As will the sun and rain,
To render all decay
Seminal, in time
For soft winds of promise,
And outpouring blooms
In springtime's sweet air.
Cosmic voices do speak.
Have you not heard them keen?

III.

Advocates of tranquility,
Progenitors of peace,
People of consideration,
Champions of diplomacy
In chambers of worldly courts,
Do well to stem the tides of war,
For rivers of blood will follow
Hasty, ill-considered action.
A nation sorely needs such souls,
For consequences matter here.
Right action cannot yield to rhetoric
When facts lend themselves to cause;
Therefore, let all speak of grievances
For truth's sake, free of private gain
And unsullied by treacherous talk.

One day, if by chance, opposition
Triumphs in argumentation,
Let the just cause justly prevail.

IV.

The screaming city rocks;
It totters and crumbles.
Solemn faces scramble
From fire to ashen dust
To account for loved ones;
They dare not shriek aloud
For fear of fear itself.
Some flee, and others crawl,
Age indiscernible:
The hunt for life is on.
It was once a beautiful
Lover's promenade,
Aflame with desire
Under the cool moon eye;
Now shovels do not cease
To pry the new caverns
For the trapped and the maimed,
Or even a faint cry.

V.

The beloved country
Stands strong against the foe,
And all know sacrifice.
One cannot flee from fate.
The air is cold, food scarce,
But we manage on grass,
And, if need be, eat weeds.
We do not speak of war;
We do not speak of loss.
We are a stalwart lot,
And await better times

With equanimity.
Sirens blare across town;
Sentries patrol, others scurry,
And shelters come alive.
Someone strikes up a song;
We know it well, and sing.
It will be a long night.

VI.

The children are hungry;
They wail out of weakness,
With no remedy in sight.
Our desperation grows.
They are our very life,
And we cannot lose them.
The old and infirm ail
With noble forbearance,
But some elect to die;
This is indeed bitter,
For they mean to spare us.
In dark days such as these,
We cannot care for pets,
And this, too, is trying.
We layer our clothing,
Huddle for body heat,
Take turns at telling tales,
And so, pass the night
As in Boccaccio.

VII.

Each dawn brings with it new hope,
And each night, the weary sleep
In a realm of shattered dreams,
Where heavy hearts haunt rubble
In search for what is not found.
One's shadow haunches over,

And the sun is blotted out.
Remembering is costly,
And it kills those who grieve.
Blank. Be blank. Defeat longing.
In hell, think not of heaven;
Inure yourself; steel yourself;
One day, you will laugh again;
You will have a life again.
Console yourself; lift your eyes.
Days roll into weeks, then months;
Torpor and disease set in.
With the end so near, we know
Not everyone will make it.

How Bloodless the Sound

Collateral damage:
Now, here we have a phrase,
A new phrase on the tongue,
A tough phrase, hard to chew,
Hard to swallow, and hard to digest;
A phrase designed to assuage
Conscience or abate alarm,
A phrase to still the heart
Or outcry of indignation;
A phrase to diminish,
A phrase to mislead,
And a phrase to destroy
The force of the unthinkable;
A phrase to open the door
To a daring entitlement:
To forge ahead with it,
And to distance one's self
From dire consequences:
To use it as a buffer,
A coating, a means

Of justification,
A hardening of feeling,
An assertion, if you will,
That the inert: a structure,
A desk, an office, a canister
Perhaps, may be equated
With a child, a mother, a man,
And equally to be disposed of
In limp lives and severed limbs.
Sadly, collateral damage
Does exist: it is real enough.
If "A," then "B." How simple
The rule of logic can be,
And *boom*: life is expendable
In service to ideology.
It is the triumph of method,
And a calm mind gone mad.

Still Life

A lifetime of not knowing;
A lifetime of faded photographs.
Beautiful people in family groups,
Baby in arm, mother seated,
Father protectively behind a chair,
One outstretched arm a shield
Incapable of safeguarding a soul
In the black and white glossy—
All of it frozen in time.

Nona's face is tranquil;
Her hair is pulled back,
And her forehead is adorned.
A band we take to be silver
Stretches across her brow.

It may well be a crown;
She is a regal woman
Who exudes steadfastness.
Nonu stands behind her
Tall, handsome and bearded.

The women are stunning
Brunettes with almond eyes
Meant for the adoration
Of the beloved destined
To perhaps die in the woods
They walked in as lovers.
Perhaps they died as partisans,
Kissed or held hands under the moon,
Went to the camps, or drowned,
Cast adrift in an act of arch malice.
They were certainly murdered.

Elegy

This is an elegy
It mourns; it grieves;
It unsettles the heart.
It is tender, it is pained,
It is loving,
It is full of tears
That cannot be assuaged.
A beautiful girl,
A beloved child,
Adored and adorned,
Cherished and held high
In the arms of love,
Perishes
In the suffocating
Airs of death-dealing
Swirls of sadism's

Masterwork,
But in memory's vault
The distillation
And triumph
Of unforgettable beauty
Remains.

Modern Times

The airplane shrieks
Across a pained sky
And shutters quiver
Across the many rooms
None will live in again;
The clock records the rounds
In mute, unthinking precision,
And the crescendo
Of humming cars
Assault the ozone-charged air
Through slaughtered paths
Buried under concrete.
Blood, body, bone and stone
Rot and fuse; the noxious air
Corrodes the spirit,
And precipitous thoughts
Hurtle past gray zones
Of steel, concrete, and fallen beams
To rest upon the naked earth
Violated, all innocence gone.

The Roll of Thunder

In times of peril,
If we dare to hope
Or care to act,
What course can we take
When sanity lies
Under prolonged siege,
And the first bodies
Of rampage appear
To the amazed eye,
Unblinking, on watch,
As everyday events
Unfold in candor?
Does anyone know
What right conduct is,
When lives are at stake?
If the many are mad,
Consumed by ardor
For the newest rage,
And that is the norm,
Will it not be the few
In opposition
Who will be routed
By the herding crowd?
Who will hear a word
Of what they have to say
When they are cut off?
However they cry:
"Calamity claims
The most innocent
Singly or in hordes
As the first victims
Or pawns of power,
And wretchedness will
Follow,
Disease and hunger
Will follow,

Rape and savagery
Will follow,"
Will any take heed?
Any remember?
A single voice heard
Can roll like thunder.

The Adventure

One learns to think
About consequences;
The said and unsaid
Have power
To create and destroy,
Augment evil,
Or endow the sound,
But how can one know
If action or inaction
Fulfills or aborts
The perceived intention?

Is uncertainty a friend?
Is it a matter of choice?
Does it hold us hostage,
Or are we made observers
And merely impotent
Before the facts?
If we weigh matters,
Who balances the scale?
On whom do we rely?
Shall we leave it to intuition
Or a random gadfly?

Do we find the way
In the labyrinth
When we are lost

Or disoriented?
Do we find it in the forge
When we are fired,
Newly-shaped, and strengthened?
Is the ideal of wisdom illusory,
A comic spectacle,
Or a cosmic-wide canvas
Upon which humanity dabbles?

Deception

The fear is there;
It devours us.
Because of it,
We hunger,
Cringe, hide,
Pursue, attack,
Avenge
With conviction,
And, as a safeguard,
Beat a drum,
Wear a mask,
Wear a costume!
Wave a flag,
Drink a potion,
Offer incantations,
Purify, vilify,
Avenge,
Burn, or kill
The besieging
Force, demon,
Or phantom
We suppose
To be other
Than ourselves.

Foolish Questions

How does it feel
To stand alone
Against the mob,
Against the complacent,
Against denial,
Against fear;
Against the tide?
To see it all
Beforehand?
To see the steps
To perdition,
To calamity,
To tribulation?
To know;
To warn;
To cry;
To shout
Stand strong,
And not be heard?
How does it feel
To see the branch struck,
The tree shaken,
The house fall?
The bewildered
And the silent,
Not the first
To be taken down?
Not the first
To be battered
Awake and defenseless,
Emotions swirling?
Not the first to rail
At the earnest men,
A breed apart,
Who slay and slash,
And steer clear of carnage;

Who sweep it away?
Step aside; away, trash;
Goodbye, discard.
Too bad. Shut up.
Get used to it, baby.
Squawk, squawk, squawk.

How does it feel?
My god. Need you ask?

Questions

Is the heart
Ever forgetful,
Ever forgiving,
Ever overlooking,
Ever trusting?
Is that what you think?
Is it at the root of hope?
Is it an expanse
So wide, so ample
So all encompassing
And so unquantifiable,
That all can be waived
In a moment
And forsaken for a smile,
An embrace,
A caress,
A touch,
And yes, a kiss—
A moment's vision of paradise,
Undying innocence
Or untarnished virtue?
Is this what you believe?
What do we say
Of the untamed, untrained,

Unhinged mind?
Who speaks for reason?
Who cries "Stop,"
Like the sanest of madmen
In the stark darkness
Of night? Who
Dares oppose the avalanche,
Stem the floodtide,
Or uphold the world,
When the earth is rising
And the sky falling?
Is it you, who
Unflinchingly
Consigns and flings
The mortal capsule
Into the pyres of hell
As a burnt offering,
To tease the heavenly
Nostrils of salvation?
Is it you who
Rues yesterday's slumber
In martyred flesh?

Part Three

Vignette

A robin nestles within
The pitted path as if to be
Comforted for the loss of
That other nest she will
Never see again.

Across a redwood plank bridge,
Live oak, great rocks, and stately reeds
Hug the shore in profusion;
Crushed beer cans float listlessly
In thickly-viscous inlets of
Trapped moss,
And a solitary dragonfly darts
Between the wispy pampas grass,
Seaming it in silvery-blue streams.

A bouquet of balloons has been loosed,
And the gesture is not lost on us;
Someone understands letting go.
The colors bob in air, spreading
Like the yawning petals of a giant
Budding rose yet to be named.
Red, blue, and yellow discs spin swiftly
Across the day to canine delight,
While carousing lovers steal a kiss
And napping grandmothers abandon
Lunchtime meals on checkered cloths.

It is Sunday in the park,
Before the children tire,
The mist descends,
And familiar irritations set in.

Attaining the Heights

A tree does not sprout from a leaf,
A pyramid does not rise from a pinnacle;
A spire is not the foundation of a skyscraper,
And a dome, for any manner of forum,
Must, like all else, have a strong base.
So it is with all human endeavor
That aspires to attain the heights.

From the roots of imagination—
In dreams, as a gift of the gods
Or in thought, as a gift of the intellect—
Solitude befriends us with vision,
A fanciful notion, curious to the mind,
A moment's diversion, and pleasantry
Or dread over the unknown outcome—
But if we would behold fancy's face
As architects of the dream, we strive
With passion as an ally; we persevere,
Plan, innovate, and do the impossible
As did Beethoven. We journey far
As did Mozart; we fill the void
With light and luminous faces,
Like Vermeer, and we pay the price
In a currency greater than gold.
Find your way; find your place,
Unafraid and undeterred.
Do it like impoverished Rembrandt;
Do it like Proust, shuttered in a room,
Dosteovsky in jail and Kafka in mind
Or Chagall in love and Van Gogh in a field.
Do it like Lautrec, free of infirmity in a café,
Or the nameless valiant in the camps.
Do it; just do it for yourself. Perhaps
One day you will gladden the heart of man.

The Delayed Parting

The sun moved
Another hour
Into its orbital space,
Stretching the afternoon
Lazily across the yawning day.
Just right, I thought.
The heat has slowed
The heartbeat of time.
We could scarcely move,
Anyway. Our slumbering
Desire to say good-bye
Would awaken, but right now
The eclipse of our souls
Had not quite lined up.
It will only be a moment,
A mere matter of
Cosmic order,
Before the impervious moon
Deprives the earth of shadow,
But in that interminable
Distance between fragile moments
When worlds obscure one another
Without loss of mooring or fear,
Life will rekindle the wick
Against the close of day.

La Entrada

The morning swims in the breeze
And warbles its song past dawn;
The drone of autos begins its hum
Across the stillness of a new day,
Following it into pitch darkness
And the well-earned sleep of the weary.
A far away truth rumbles over
The roll and clatter on railroad tracks,
And a hoot, moist with mystery, shudders
And screams its greeting to the wind.

The vagabond and homeless
Signal their arrival in worn shoes,
Walking into the passage of time,
Walking into the waking city,
Walking into the lonely city
Where infrequent dreams,
Luxurious and rare,
Seek the unafraid dreamer.

I long to join travelers and transients
Into other mornings unlived in as yet,
But as my soul sits on an egg-laden nest
And thus roosts like a fine, fat hen,
My unaware heart cracks its shell,
Enters the boundlessness
With incomprehensible ease,
And pulsates with the near and far
Untroubled by distance.

At Home in Monterey Bay

I tuck a rainbow
Between my brows
And rose petals
Between my breasts,
To greet the day.

I love the solitary
Houses facing old worlds
On the edge of the sea
And steaming shacks,
Farmland barns,
Disused windmills,
Smell of sage and pine,
Shape of cypress and oak,
Quaint country church,
Adobe mission, and
One-room schoolhouse
Nestled in the aromatic grove,
Where jazz and Bach and lovers
Between the forest and the sea,
Spill gladness into the heart
Of the flowing lapis night.

With the moon to guide the tides,
Stars for coverlets, visions
Of lazing otter upon the rock,
Or spawning whale in the expanse,
I have no need for other dreams.

Stunned Speechless

Meadows of blue-green grass,
Moving fields of textured velour
And sweeping beds of dandelion
That bend to the will of the wind,
Country-place and farmhouse
Near the swift rivers, rocky cliffs,
And ancient Indian trails,
Dark forests, tumescent with dew,
The splendor of sunlight prisms,
Towering pine and stately birch,
Wildflower and weed, cow-dung
Clusters and well-worn paths,
Subterranean gopher holes, tunnel sites,
Whippoorwill trills, swallowtail flight,
Splash of robin breast or marauding bluebird—
Blue skies and gathering clouds,
Rain-soaked winds and snows from above,
Majestic choreography
That daily sweeps before the eye
And converges on the destined prey,
The swoop of pelican grace; the
Fallen bird in playful cat's jaw
And mewing kittens pawing life,
Trembling and rustling leaves,
Dancing bees that inseminate
In quivering, soft, flower deeps,
Span of the spider's dew-glistened web,
Touch of the leeches' kiss, and
Hissing snakes that groom the grass
In the cool, cool underbrush
Still the mind, and silence the beholder.

The Lark

He is shallow;
You know that.
He is unconscious;
You know that.
He is for himself;
You know that.
He is parasitic;
You know that.
He is irresponsible;
You know that.
He is a hedonist;
You know that too.
He is an anarchist;
And you know this.
He is immoral;
And this.
He is amoral;
And this too.

Is he bitter?
Yes.
Is he frightened?
Yes.
A fallen angel?
Oh yes.
Can he sing?
Yes.
And dance?
Yes.
Play the fool?
Absolutely.
Is he lost?
I'm afraid so.

Night and Day

Enveloped in arms
Under cover of night
And outside of time
In the stillness,
Wholeness of surrender
Bestows the invisible sheath of love
To eclipse imperfection.
A new reckoning awaits
The break of day,
When other truths
May be rendered
In better light,
And the sheath
Is seen as a shroud.

Beginnings

The lover within
Wears no fig leaf.
Naked in the garden
Of unnamed apples,
A slithery thing
Soon to be named,
Furrows the soil
For a new plot,
But here and now,
There is only me.
Nature opens
Its arms
To greet itself.
It is the first
Awakening.

Part Four

Birthday

She was born at Christmastime
Eve or day, she knew not which,
And so, we rounded the bend;
We celebrated it all,
As the grandest of birthdays.
It was not incidental,
But rather fortuitous
That mankind shared it with her,
For she believed in omens,
Talismans and remedies,
Incantations, and magic
To thwart the envious eye
And corroding suspicion.

She believed she was special
To have a day set apart—
A day of festivity
And sober contemplation
Inspired by the hope for peace
And the suspension of war,
For she knew the ravages
That attend calamities
Served by war and invasion;
She knew them well as a child
Whose parents fled to safety,
Hoping to prepare the way
For the children left behind.

The longing that stirred her heart,
The love that eluded her,
She found in the promise of
Valentino's smoldering eyes
Or love's redemptive power
As shown on every screen,
But life did not yield the prize
So desired and remote

In hard times across the land.
Joy was celluloid fiction,
And a hard lesson to learn
For a new American
Who had full faith in the dream.

Virtue

I.

Papa was a union man
In the days when
A quarter an hour
Embittered the best
And soap-box orators
Spilled the rhetoric
Of their intellect
Among the ragged,
Wretched poor
Freed for unemployment.
Bent over rent shoes
And threadbare coats
Across the friendless,
Cheerless cement,
They walked the walk
The downcast know well.
With clenched fists
And visored caps on head,
Gaunt masses listened
For news of bread,
A chance to get ahead,
Pay the rent or marry.
It was not easy to bear,
But there was something,
Something sad and strong,
Determined to get along,
That showed in their eyes.

II.

The new industrialists
Sold their apples from crates,
Unable or unwilling to cry
Mister, can you spare a dime,
As they huddled for warmth
Over fires set in drums and
Roasted potatoes or chestnuts.
Chilled to the bone, they waited
For someone, any unlikely someone,
To buy a paper or barter
A bowl of soup for an article.
The women were in the streets, too.
They lined-up at subway entries
In freshly starched cotton dresses,
Wore aprons, and cast a beseeching eye.
Dignity, need and resignation
Writ plainly on face and stance,
They bargained cautiously,
Clutched brown-bagged
Peanut-butter-and-jelly sandwiches
In odorous, clorox-tinted hands,
And worried about hungry children,
The old and sick in unheated rooms.

III.

How many absent meals make a scab?
How many abuses stop the machines?
How much piece-work, heartache,
Sweat or tears earn a dollar?
What does it take to make a thief?
Who can measure a drunkard's rage,
Suicide's plunge, or too soon a lasting sleep?
The brutal men wield clubs by day
And blackjacks by night,
The fastidious launder their money,

The honest wash their souls in lye,
The artist dips his brush in blood
And feeds on his genius
Amid rats as hungry as he.

IV.

He was a burly man, a stranger
Who labored over the climb
To our third-floor apartment.
The stairs creaked; he groaned,
And our eyes fastened on the blackjack
In his left hand, the first we had ever seen.
He is a hired hand. He has come for papa,
I thought, and so did mama. We knew;
We both knew, but we knew differently.
Death-dealing blows were instruments
That superceded bribery in persuasion,
And papa's turn had come around
To provide a poor man his dinner.
This is how one earns one's bread.
Bitter lessons awaited the worker
Who strove for better conditions,
And that certainly was my papa,
But he was not at home just then,
And this man would go hungry.
Mama stood, waiting quietly,
And the weapon's hold relaxed;
There was no one here to harm.
He was an honest man,
Not given to embellishment—
And yet, disappointment held him there,
Transfixed upon the creaking stair.
He had come far; he was tired,
And it was hard to find work.

The Womb of Loneliness

I have no job
I have no home
I have no place
I walk the streets
I have nothing
I am nothing
But a bedraggled rag
I am all alone
I am hungry
I do not eat
I am cold
I do not sleep
It rains
I am wet
It shines
I sweat
I am your tomorrow
I am your despair
Tomorrow
Today
I am your neighbor
I roll into a ball
It is the cocoon
From whence I came
And where I now die
Once I had a name
Tomorrow
They will say I am you.

Unmasking the Mask

My heart has been cast down;
It has been trampled underfoot,
And its chambers bleed.
None see this. I wear a mask,
I function well in this state,
And the show goes on.
Details do not matter;
Sight and *seeing* differ.
The surface suffices
For the rudiments
Of ordinary vision—
We see it work for the blind,
Who probe both air
And path cautiously
To skirt danger—
But I, an opera buff,
Attuned to passionate excess
And destiny's triumph over desire,
Weep unmasked at the conviction
Of an aria that sears the soul,
And treat off-stage realities
With the fiction of learnedness.

Part Five

Vida y Mar

At the sea
In Santa Maria,
Between the beach
And dolphin reality,
I stood against a cliff
Strongly holding the shore
In jagged safety.
Against its flanks,
Moss and mussels,
Clam and sea anemone
Clung deeply, too.

My feet felt the quick sands
And swirling currents
Poetically,
The azure-vaulted sky
Evoked the same from
My poetic eye,
And I sang:
Oh, concentric circles
Of eddying, tugging waters
Ever downward in your swift course,
What philosophy in this, your force?

I have not swum at sea,
But this is enough for me,
Thought I, and I stood my ground
Around the cutting edge of the
Ominous shelf, now darkening,
Now settling into its demonic face.
The lash of whipped waters
Slashed across my body,
The swells rose, the sea swirled,
And icy pellets of piercing frost
Assaulted me in the cold, cold sea.
It was time to leave, but I could not go.

The sea played with me,
Ripping me
Into sweeping vasts
Within whose troughs
I was cradled for moments,
And I looked up in wonder
At the seething, breathing sea
That would teach me
Unrelentlessly,
The facts of its nature
As it crashed into power
Across my aching chest
And overawed eyes.

I prepared myself and watched
The descending foam emptiness
In the arc of a wave. I beheld
The majestic, billowing softness
As it smothered me beneath its frothy mass
In snow-like, luridly-living , Japanese
Woodblock prints of frozen reality,
And too busy to die badly,
I looked on in Zen awareness.

Thinking I would be meat
For generations of worms,
I was mightily consoled
To feed the fish who had fed me.
The sun shone; the sea sparkled
Past thunderous volumes
That urged me on to the horizon,
And thrashed me into the depths.
I would soon be no more,
And I had no cause for complaint.
Raising my hand to salute the shore,
My thoughts soared: *Farewell, adieu,*
Goodbye. These are my last moments.
Children were at play, parents scolded,

Men walked the sandy beach and looked
Out to sea, but none looked out for me.

Thus, nearing the end,
A great bard came to the fore,
And I, now ready, eased
Into my watery bed
Without a garland.
What? No seaweed? No kelp
To crown my unadorned head?
This cannot be, smile I inwardly,
Little dreaming to succeed myself
Like a beached cork or missive
To the safety of the shore,
Bearing the sea within me.

La Tia

The madwoman drove
Across her Via Dolorosa
Through vast Inca wastes,
Distracted by visions
Of immanent betrayal.

Who shall it be? *Who*?
"Who shall slay me,"
She asked proudly. . .
"Is it he? *is it he*
is it he is it, oh god?"
Her mad mind whispered,
Moving through marvels
Onto martyred lips
Attracted by terror.
Judas, where are you?
Look. Look here! Look at my face!
Look from this side, and this.

See the chin, the profile!
"Do they know me? Do *they?*
Have *they* recognized me?
Mira y habla, buen hombre!
LOOK and *SPEAK, GOOD MAN!*
I am the reformer,
And Judas will come.

A cigarette dangled between
Her lips, deep in ecstasies' throes
And cocaine-inspired Pisco talk.
She twirled and flung her outstretched arms,
Awaiting the validation,
And it seemed to her it had come.
"Mira, mira. Mira a mia corona!"
The luminous moon and a myriad stars
Had fallen over the Andean land,
And the expanse of the village was
Indeed a crown for any Christ.

Las Madres de los Disparacedos

She is an outlet to the sea
She is the breadth of horizon
The azure night filled with stars
A luminous moon and planet
Among unexplored worlds
She is nature itself
Being itself in the long
Lonely arc of night
When sad recall seeks redress
And she cannot sleep or rest
Until her heart is set aright

She is a woman, a mother,
An indefatigable force;
She is a pillar, a lioness
Looking for the lost cub;
She is a mountain, bursting,
Red hot in indignation.
She is a league on the march,
An army without arms,
Demanding accountability,
Protesting the tyrannical
Complicit with corruption,
Protesting the blind eye, deaf
Ear, and bald, daring hypocrisy
That strips the lair by stealth,
Slays its protector, and claims
The pride as its very own.
She seeks the child of her child
And the child of her friend's child,
The disappeared, unknowing,
And orphaned children,
Fated to reckon with poseurs,
Fraudulent parents all, fraught
With guile or guilt or a lust
Of unconscionable depravity.

She will bring them back,
And she is bringing them back.
The heavens, once more in orb,
Restore to its rightful bosom
The child of the child that is no more.

Lima de Dia

The cement steams; the senses reel.
The vapors of purgatory belch across
The equatorial streets of Lima, a place
Where jostling hordes and quarreling vendors
Vie with the theater of inspired hawkers,
Plagues, and indigents bargaining
For a sole's worth of tomorrow's papaya.

A mime chalks his face,
And with uncanny grace
Spellbinds a mass of men
Who create a magic circle
For miracles to enter.

In awe of art
And with mouths agape,
The shabbily-dressed partake
Of David's triumph over Goliath,
And laugh at the mime's mockery
Of the lewdness inspired in a chaste priest
At the confessional, or turn to stone
As a crescendo of malevolence
Roars to a stop in a penitent's ear—
And all this, without a sound.

Grim as death,
Art instructs the poor
About the avarice of those
Who vowed to be poor
For God's sake.

The cement steams, the senses reel,
The vapors of purgatory exude.
These are the streets of equatorial Lima,
Where jostling hordes or quarreling vendors

Will sell you anything as they vie
In the theater of life and its sorrows.

Hot tar glistens in an angry-black glare
As squatting mothers, black derbies in place,
Drape infants to their sagging breasts and cry
Buy a baby; put my pastries to the test!
Have a liquado; try an emoliente!
Or bargain for a sole's worth of tomorrow's
Papaya, avocado, or snakeskin oil.

The palace guards place funereal tokens
On independent thought with black boots,
Bayonet in hand, saber at the side;
The helicopters lower and blot out the sun,
Shattering glass and pock-marking cafes;
The pantomimist notes the lewdest acts
Of all for tomorrow's account of today's truth,
And so begins a new day in which dreams
Get lost and black magic has its sway.

Geraldo

"Be good," she said,
But he was good as gold.
"Change," she said;
"You must change."
He bent right,
And he bent left.
He wanted to be good;
He wanted to change.
"Heart! Put your heart
Into it," she said.
He went north,
And he went south.
He toiled across the land
With pickaxe and shovel,
Jackhammer and trowel
For the elusive good—
For the change of heart—
For the mysterious arrival
Of the awaited day
When he would at last
Be greeted with a smile
Or the outstretched arms
Of the promised embrace—
But even as he awaited
The moment of grace,
Even as he said:
"No hay problema!
Solo la muerte
No puedemos trocar,"
The heart he had—
The heart he knew best
And most denied—
Ached to be free
On the cliffs of Michoacan.

Part Six

Spiritas Mundi

Open are your unprobing eyes,
Unblinking, devoid of surprise.
Freed of restraint, freed of complaint,
Parted lips that move no more,
Once moved through dreams
And childhood's kaleidoscopic door
To a womanly place, where,
Quivering in the innocence
Of but a few summers' yearning,
Maidenhead unsealed its honeycomb
In the lock of a lover's arms.

Oh lady, good lady,
You were young, but were you fair?
Did anyone matter, anyone care?
You, who now lie dead to desire,
Upon whom did that chin rest,
Whom inspire?
How well did you see,
And in whom delight,
Before immortality
Closed eyes to sight?

Oh lady, good lady,
If the great silence
That swallows the good night
Could open its mouth,
And release its jaws
To repair a tongue
Now severed from words and men,
Of whom would you speak?
With whom would you share?
In the golden sunlight,
When you counted time
In womanly days,
With whom did you laugh

In fields of springtime blossoms,
And autumnal colors of falling leaves?
For whom did you cry
In the lonely beds
Of wakeful nights and shadowy days?

Oh lady, good lady,
Though you be absent, you are not gone—
For I can see you now, in that other state,
Where songs and tears and laughter flow
In waves of joy borne of sweet pleasure
Amid the tall grass, mountains, and streams
Where waking dreams soar their winged way
To nests no condor may follow;
I can see you as you were, with a rainbow garland
In your hair, and a necklace of dewdrops
To adorn beauteous breasts that greet the dawn.

Visitation

He held me
Without a touch,
And he kissed me
With his eyes;
He moved me
Without stirring,
And he helped me
Without a hand;
He rocked me
Within the bosom
Of a smile,
Sheltered me
Within the ark
Of an embrace,

And entered my soul
Without penetration.
His breath
Is a sweet fragrance
Embossed upon
The vapors of a dream,
And no, he does not walk
Upon the waters.

Elchanan

My mind seeks the beloved.
Where is he? Everywhere?
My heart seeks the beloved.
Among whom may he be found?
Everyone? The silence reigns.
Can you help me, friend?

When last I saw him,
His eyes sank into the awesome center.
Into the dark night of unmixed feeling,
Down, down, they sank in fleeting farewell,
Like drowning lights on a gallant ship.
I saw him soar to greet the great stars;
I felt their fiery tremor in awe
As they moved galaxies for him
And I, nearer at hand, trembled, too.

The beloved left a sheath;
He left a mechanism,
A laboriously breathing body,
But it was not he;
I swear it was not he,
And I look for him.

Can you help me, friend?
Anyone? Where shall I go?
Which constellation shall I seek
Across spectacular arrays
Of pulsating stars?
Can you say? For that is the way.
That is the path to the beloved.

Tribute to Dylan

And love shall write no obituaries.
The mountains shall salt the earth
And the seas shall salt the earth
And the earth shall still be sweet.
Peppertree and sagebrush,
Dittany, rosemary, and thyme
Will scatter their smells as an offering
To all the eons without litanies,

And love shall write no obituaries.
Although dinosaur and trilobite be gone,
The earth is not forlorn; the earth is not forlorn.
Tar pits remain, and molds remain,
And fossils still tell their tales.
Scavengers may scan the skies, sweep the seas,
Or maraud the unprotected lair,
But the earth is not bare; the earth is not bare.
Through ages of ice and ages of fire
Love has given life desire,

And love shall write no obituaries.
Species emerge and species submerge,
And species adapt new ways;
The finch is not alone.
Amphibians still roam in elegance
And reptiles still groom the earth.

Dolphins sing in watery depths,
Exciting greater ambition in men,
And the great white whale still spawns her regal brood,
Trumpeting her triumph in a seawater crown,

And love shall write no obituaries.
Although Cro-magnon be gone and Neanderthaler be gone.
Cave-dwelling paintings still live on,
And the tale of hunt and herd, corral,
The gods and immortality goes on; the tale goes on.
Although the pharaohs are gone,
And the Maya and Inca are gone,
The pyramids live on and the temples live on;
Stonehenge and Machu Piccu and their mystery remain,
And the majestic Urubamba still etches the terraced Andes.

And love shall write no obituaries.
The sun shall cool, the stars shall fade,
And planet and satellite shall wax and wane;
New names shall be found to cover the ground
In other solar systems and in other galaxies,
In other times when new calendars will be written,
And the then-men will wonder about us.

The Tip of the Iceberg

When reason cedes to bias,
And wondrous cities fall;
When power beats its drum,
And famine opens its jaw;
When rivers swim in slime,
And seas murmur of death;
When industry blinds its eye,
And contaminants swirl;
When hordes are on the move,
And hot sands singe the soul;
When innocence is lost,
And vast gardens languish;
When sea lions are beached,
And whales no longer thrive,
Where will you weigh in
On the scales of blame?

Lovesong

When dreams no longer
Retain their reality,
I shall cease loving you.
When the sun revolves
Around the earth
And the moon turns ashen,
I shall cease loving you.
When stars abandon the sky
And snowflakes shed their stars,
Then, and then alone,
Shall I cease loving you.

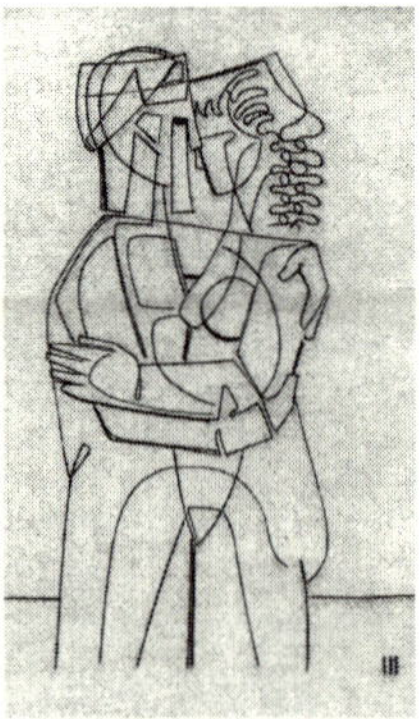

When hummingbirds' wings molt
And whales surrender their spouts,
I shall cease loving you.
When the ant is freed of necessity
And moths no longer seek the light,
Or caterpillars emerge from cocoons
And spiders no longer weave webs,
I shall cease loving you.
When bees abandon hive and queen
And turtles no longer seek the hot sands
Or dolphins cease to soar, sing, or smile
And vultures hatch hens' eggs,
Then, and then alone,
Shall I cease loving you.

When children no longer laugh
And sages abandon wisdom,
I shall cease loving you.
When magicians' sleeves
Cannot be worn by all men
And fairy tales lose their truths,
I shall cease loving you.
When all songs are silenced,
All color lost—all promises broken—
Or deceit ennobles the depraved
And machines bleed, men corrode,
Time ceases to exist, and worlds vanish—
Then, and then alone,
Will my inconstant heart
Love you no more.

When a Small-time Woman Blows her Horn

I'm a rag-time woman,
I'm a jazz-time woman,
I'm a woman who can sing;
I'm a can-can-woman,
I'm a waltzing woman,
I'm a woman who can swing.
I'm a plied woman; I'm a tried woman;
I'm a glad woman; I'm a had woman;
I'm something!

I'm a Puccini woman—*ah for Tosca;*
I'm a Nijinsky woman—*oh for the rose,*
Incurably a Martha Graham woman—
Whom else, no one knows.
I'm a mandolin woman,
Surely a violin woman—
Paganini, Lalo—and all virtuoso!
I'm a woman who can beat the drum,
Toot horns, clash cymbals or trill,
But Haydn and Bach give me a thrill.

I'm a rhapsodic woman—a harmonic,
Ecstatic, prophetic, kinetic, aesthetic,
Emphatically-erratic, charismatic woman.
I'm verbose, morose, appallingly gross,
Inclement, and always in ferment—
I'm redundant, terse, and much worse:
I'm a pietistic woman, an irreverent woman,
A proud, priggish, ethereal, material,
Sublime and surreal woman
Of great humility.

I'm a devious woman; a mischievous woman,
A Da Vinci, Pieta and Rembrandt woman,
Who would die windowless without Vermeer.
I'm a country woman; I'm a city woman;
I'm a woman of lakes and streams, open seas,
Snow-capped mountains and sheltered valleys,
Stormy nights of clapping thunder and lightning,
Etched skies, easy winds, and falling leaves.
I'm a woman of fireplaces, marshmallows and song,
Steamy cafes, soft talk in dark corners, chess
And evening walks with a dog at her heels—
Quiet pleasures, all.

I'm a radical woman; I'm a conservative woman;
I'm a woman of considerable moderation.
I'm wise; I'm silly,
Knowledgeable and incorrigible—
A woman of ranges; a woman of changes—
A perfectly stable woman.
I'm cold; I'm bold; defiant and pliant,
Tame and wild, a lady and a child—
A woman of shawls and laces,
And dozens of different faces.
I'm tender, I'm tough,
All-right, up-tight, and just right;
A giant, a pygmy, and simply me.

Sensibility

I am here,
I tell you;
I miss nothing.
Viscera,
All organs
And digits
Check in,
Accounted for.
I hear and see
And smell
The perfumed air's
Playful dance
Upon the leaf,
A wooing bird's song
Trilling through the mist
Is not lost at dawn,
Nor is nesting twig-
Gathering time.
A squirrel's greedy jaws
Gulping grape on the vine
Or reeling drunkenly,
Sated at last,
Makes me laugh,
And the robin's success
With the worm
Still struts the grassy knoll
Of my mind.
As you can see,
My work does not suffer.
My home is clean;
The cloth is laid,
The table is set,
And prosy foodstuffs
Are in place.
Why then
Is your absence
Nearer to me
Than all these?

The Goad

The sea was cold on that memorable day;
The currents were swift, the pools eddying,
The cliffs ominous—barnacle-encrusted,
Grey and dark, sharp-edged, and ancient—
But the sands of Santa Maria were white hot
Under the cool blue untroubled sky.

Venture with me, be not afraid,
My blithe muse beckoned. Dare
To breach the unknown depths—
And his beauty shone on that day
As never before.

The grandeur of a snow-capped mountain
Beckoned on a sparkling day in early spring;
The lodge, huge and cozy, heavily-laced
In drifts of hot chocolate and coffee,
Oozed with warmth amid the cracklings
Of forsaken woods ablaze in an ample fireplace.

Venture with me, be not afraid,
My blithe muse beckoned. Dare
To discover the sweep of the slopes—
And his hubris won on that day
As never before.

I did not swim and I could not ski
On two days, continents apart,
And of what consequence is that?
I shall never forget the depths
And majesty of the mountain,
Or the wonder of being alive.

Return Passage

You come back to me
In ways I do not expect,
In ways I cannot expect
Religious truths to manifest.
It moves me to see
Your once-dead eyes rise
From under entombed lids.
In ashen agony, you squint
Before the unaccustomed light
To pierce a moment's reality.
It is hard for you to give up
The small comforts of ignorance
So late in the day.
An hour ago you were
Invincibly young,
Not at all an ordinary man.

Homage

There was tenderness—
That is true—
And because we touched it,
It touched us as we lay
In one another's arms,
I, with my head tucked
Under your armpit, my
Hand holding the storing
Places of your generations
And you, enfolding me,
Tugging me, assuring me
To lean your way in love,
Glowing with knowledge,
Glowing with moonlight,
Glowing with a smile,
I, your sun; you, my moon—

You, my sun; I, your moon
Glowing, glowing, glowing;
Aura upon aura, radiating.
To be timeless in the moment?
We knew that.
To be one amidst division?
We knew that.
To be naked and yet dressed
In the raiment of existence?
We knew that too—
But that was long ago,
Before division
Separated us forever.

The Catalyst

He walks the streets
At twelve o'clock
In the afternoon
And I walk that mile with him,
Steadying the course
Of an imperfect love,
Happy that through him
At last, I can love
All fallible men.

The Forge

A chisel hammers into the soul
Something of the new day's madness;
The lunancy of unreason encircles
A forlorn globe in glib rhetoric.

To the Indulgent

Run by the tropical shore,
Ride the wave, skirt the surf,
Hear the song of the gray whale,
Swim, play golf, and make love
In pineapple-scented fields
On lazy afternoons.
When the sun gives way
To the drift of the sea
Brushing the cool breeze
Across your brow, lie
Beneath the undulating palm;
Let desire rise, and siesta fall
Anew in another's arms.
Pluck an apple from the laden tree
Beckoning from the dizzying branch,
Resist certain knowledge,
And await the night's revelry:
A dance, a throbbing drum,
A thumping heart, a kiss.
The promise of conquest,
And new night labors.
Whet the appetite of old bones,
With a flourish close to courage.

Reversal

He was ill, he was rash,
And he heaved as he breathed,
His rasping voice a shock
Of rumbling eruptions,
His face a distortion,
A mask of ghostly hue.
The day, blizzard cold,
Chilled him to the bone
And he coughed frightfully,
Wounding the ill-served words
Colliding in mid air.
Misconstruing illness
To be subservient
To the force of his will,
He dared the elements
To crush him if they could.

A wan smile slashed his lips
As destiny took hold
To thwart undertaking
So bold and mad a step
As he contemplated.
A chance meeting with fate,
That is all that it was—
And life was not squandered.
Did he learn anything?
Is that what you would know?
It took a while, my friend.
Life has plans of its own.
A consuming boredom
Had assailed him too soon.
The wild play, the bold boast,
The abandoned sickbed
Were what he returned to,
But not as he had dreamed.

Moroccan Monologue

The heaps bothered me, and I didn't like them at all. What were they doing there, anyway? This was a public place, and far from clean. You know how it is: people aren't very careful. In any case, the laundry belonged elsewhere and, at the very least, it deserved a basket, a beautiful thing made of straw. *Oh oh.* I couldn't believe my eyes. What was that idiot up to? *Was he blind?* The truth is the laundry bothered me a lot. This man is crazy, I thought. He's going to spit right there! *Hey, Mister*! My God, how do you say that here? *You don't; you don't. You don't say anything like it, either.* Mister, Mister, be careful. It's so clean! I've nev-er seen anything like it Mister, so please, please don't. I was very disturbed. Who would leave laundry like that untended? It made no sense! Oh of course the man spit. He spit more than once and missed each time, but that was a miracle. Well, you can imagine how I felt. I didn't like this man at all. The fact is, I hated him on the spot, but what could I do? There was just me, and so I spit at him with all my mind. I spit and I spit and I spit, until I drenched him. *Ha! Ha!* Ha, Ha. Good. That'll teach him! Can you imagine how wonderful I felt? It's useless to argue with me. I said I gave the man a bath, and I did! *What happened to him?* He walked away, and that was that. The laundry was safe and I was happy, but imagine my surprise when someone else came up to the sheets and began talking to them. Talking, I tell you! He didn't say much and he spoke real low, but in no time at all, the laundry moved. Now I had seen everything. You don't believe me. I've gone too far perhaps, but I understand you, my friend. You did not offend me—not at all—but let me go on. *Where was I?* Oh yes. The sheets began to move. It couldn't be, but there it was. The laundry got up on its feet. What a sight! An arm thrust itself out of the bundle, swept one of the sheets over its head, and clenched it between its teeth. Down came the grip! The animal had sprung its own trap. A look of ferocious intensity now came over the creature, as I trembled and turned to stone. Gone were the almond eyes and high brow, the olive skin and jeweled nostril. Gone were the youngish face and blue-black braids. The laundry had come to life; it was, after all, a woman—and once again, she vanished into the sheets. The man moved on, straight as an arrow, as she paced herself behind him, hobbling a bit. I looked at her as she trailed him for a long, long time, until, at last, her garments joined the horizon and filled the screen of the moment before the blazing sun set.

Comedia

I love you.
You know
That I love you.
I know that you know,
And you know that I know.
The fact is, you love me, too.
We both know what we know,
And what is more,
We know that it is true.
How is it, then,
That so much knowledge
Produces so little wisdom?

When Alone, the Heart Speaks

Tomorrow I will be strong,
But tonight belongs to me
And immeasurable sorrow,
Heart breaking sorrow,
Deep sorrow, feeding on
Itself sorrow; sorrow within
Sorrow, sorrow, knowing
Love isn't enough sorrow;
Knowing one has known; that
One has long known
The situation sorrow;
That there are no surprises
Sorrow; none. None at all,
And so sad; so sad to be right
Sorrow; so sorry not to be
Mistaken sorrow. Sorrow so
Deep a sorrow that I dissolve
Into the tears that cannot
Escape from the source
Of the sorrow.

Who is the Architect of a Dream?

Who is the architect of a dream?
What is the inspiration for the will?
Why does the solitary one
Oppose the stream?
All worthy questions,
Are answerable,
But these are not.
Is it perhaps an inferno
Without a flame
That warms the heart
And fires the mind?

A need to, if not actually climb
The mountain, however steep,
To do so with all one's passion
In a consummate
Act of imagination?
Is it a sound, perhaps?
The highest, most tremulous,
Deepest, most penetrating
Wrenching of the anguished soul,
That moved us at another's grief?
Anger? Hate? Revenge? *Mori! Mori!*
Cries Tosca; *Mimi!* wails Alfredo;
Gilda, Mia Gilda, the splintered
Soul of Rigoletto bewails.
A terrible irony in justice,
And straightaway we are petrified,
Filled with remorse, or in awe
Of art's searing intensity?
Are we reminded
That we long ago
Forgot how to feel,
And now see such loss
As to make us plot our course
Against the wind?
Whom do we admire,
And whom loathe?
Does it matter at all,
Or is it simply
That we have finally
Understood
We have work to do,
And our voices are needed?

Part Seven

The Copout

Where shall the
Arrow of my soul
Fly, if not to the
Heart of itself?
All directions lead
There. None is
Extraneous.
I remind myself
Each digression
Tames the jungle
Of my mind,
But it is often
After the fact,
And eminently
Human to excuse it
As such.
Don't you agree?

The Game

Please
Let me understand this:
You wish to play the game
Of the cat with the mouse.
Is that right? Well, is it?
Ah ha! It is, isn't it?
Now I see. Oh dear,
Poor fellow,
Are you certain
You will be the first cat?

Take a step.
The river is cold.

Take a step.
The river is swift.

Take a step.
The river is turgid.

Take a step;
The river is the river.

•

At the moment
I feel like singing
Many songs to keep
The long night company,
But first, I think
I will light a candle
In the dark, so that
It will not fear
The shadows of men
Or be accosted by stealth.

•

It seems as if I am doing this,
But I am doing that,
And even that is not so—
At least, not completely.

This is not entirely
A mystery.

From gurney to gurney
Across the white curtain
Barrier, I heard
A believing woman's
Unlocked and unloosed heart
Address the ultimate,
And I have called her plaint
The Emergency Room
Blues

Oh Lord, I'm so tired;
Oh Jesus, I'm so cold.
I want to go to the rest room.
Lord, I'm down here!
Oh Lord, I am not so old.
I'm seventy-four. I was young
At twenty-five,
I got a friend who's ninety.
I got no socks *down there.*
You get me some socks!
I'm cold!
Oh boy. Oh, oh.
That's good, Oh Lord.
Oh Lord. Oh Jesus.
I have to cover.
I want some socks!
I don't know what I've done,
Oh Lord. I need glasses.

Are you surprised
That I am affected
By you?

No.

Are you surprised
That I care?

No.

Does anything surprise you?

No.

•

I am
Weak,
Near death,
Vulnerable,
Naked,
Limp,
And
Disheartened.
The sobriety
Of it all
Is enough
To kill me.

•

well, there's no use denying
that we're all fools and that
the lot of us need a bit of a
washing and time in the sun;
just a bit of color and warmth
should do it and, oh yes, no
shame over the naked truth.

I could have
Killed you then;
I could have smashed
The brittle glass
You had become,
And ground it down,
Pulverizing everything
Into the powdery dust
People sneeze at,
But I withheld my hand.
I am not sorry,
And I am not glad;
It was not my work.

•

Flames
Lift
Their tongues
And lick the air,
Tasting nothing.
How wantonly
A whispering glow
Eases into tomorrow.
Burning at the undersides
Of now,
A new day is borne
By red hot embers.

The orchestration
Of solitude
Swells within,
And I feel it tuning up;
The signs are very clear
As the parts check in.
The dreary day ahead
Will bring no respite;
Clouds sail across the sky
. . . Indications of rain
Batter the brain. . . .
When will they burst;
When will they fall?
When will they open
To a fresher outlook
Where late dust is swept
Under the cosmic rug?
Will the wind be the first
To whisper what it knows?

•

Out of the abyss,
A kiss for me.
Unsought,
The prize sought me
And, there,
In the darkened
Recesses of mind,
The prisms
Of a
Flaming jewel
Light the labyrinth.

•

Your face sweeps before me,
Brushing love's joy aside;
Your gestures move in the wind
And find feet with which to dance.
A panorama of ecstasy and pain
Lifts the blinds on my aching eyes.
So alive on winter's edge?
I would bury you if I knew how.

•

I find my seat,
I know the place.
It has been waiting
Above the gleaming sea,
Upon a promontory
Facing East.
A wind-etched rock
Draws me into its lap,
I spread velour
Over the hard cradle,
The earth eases me,
And I sink into stone.

•

I wanted to hold
My friend,
But he had a fever
And I withdrew;
I wanted to caress
My friend,
And I could not.
Am I too pure,
Or not pure enough?
Come, open the door
Of my ignorance,
For I am feverish, too.
Will you hold my hand?

I thought
I was prepared
For the touch
Of your eyes;
I had felt them
So often.
From across
A great distance
They fastened
On me.
A door
I had not known
Was closed
Unlocked,
And you entered
Like a thief.

You cut a rose
From my garden
And brought it to me
Between your fingers.
My heart smiled
At the gift,
And warmed to you
As the giver
Who achieved all
In the gesture
Of completion.

It is no use;
There is no escape.
I will be with you
In other realities,
Where rainbows bridge
What cannot be touched,
Or elsewhere,
By cool streams
And waterfalls.
Look for me
In rock pools,
Where sea anemone cling
To the ocean's edge,
Sand crab burrow
Among gelatinous jellyfish,
And sandpipers scurry
Across the washed shores
Of the continent.
A long time from now,
We will be everywhere
And everything to
One another,
Just as we are now.

We piss in the wind,
Don't we?
And yet, the wind
Takes no revenge.
It is simply in
The nature of things
That we get slapped
In the face
By virtue of our acts.

My muse strikes me
In the morning
When I am uncovered,
Naked, in full mortality,
And the ordinary clocks
Have been punched in.
When I think about it,
I know I am weary.
It seems only yesterday
That I toiled in other fields
Like a drone whose every motion
Dances to measure the next day's
Cache of golden honey.
To whom shall nectar, so
Sweetly gathered in the sun
Be dear? Do you know?
Will you savor? Please?
Will you? Or you?
It is free, you know.
Is that too much?

•

Safe
In the harbor
Of your sorrows,
Will you venture
The deep sea?
I think of this,
My friend.
How will it go
With you
In the shallow
Port
Where dreams
Do not
Lift anchor?

Portrait

The red kite
Takes to air,
Jutting
Now right, now left
In slow ascent.
All cheek, all jaw,
And no eye,
An instrument of the wind
Dances to its tune.

Tail and string
Aid the upward path
Until, soaring past
The highest limbs,
It drifts in lighter
Atmosphere, released
By the child who raced
To make it fly.
The earthly hold is loosed
In knowing homage
To those who sail
Without charting a course,
Unfeeling, unseeing, and yet,
Yielding to elemental force.

The friend
Awakens late;
What may have happened
Does not matter.
Having thrown caution
To the wild and free
Gypsy airs of change,
I am happy for her.
Richly-impoverished
Of mind,
A wealth of wonder
Restores everything.

•

These gardens
Need watering,
My daughter;
They thirst
For the tilt
Of your head,
The tip of your nose,
The arch of your neck.
Your eyelids and
The brush of your hair
Bring renewal
And a new fragrance
For thorns to ponder.

Tears flow.
Sight unseen,
The heart breaks
Without lesions;
It bleeds
In composure.
Sorrow sinks
The stricken soul,
Breath ebbs
Slowly at first,
And then,
It is quite still.
Transfixed,
Aquiver
In memory
Alone,
Its beauty
A mystery,
One smiles
With eyes askance.

Point Reyes
A Place for Kings

I sit upon the scraggly brush
Near an unused trail
With mythic stuff before my eyes
In the arc of the ocean,
Sweep of the sea, and old
Oak tree overseers
High on the ancient hill.
Accepting without surprise,
I still wonder why sparrows
Do not venture the mountain
Amidst shrieking gulls, the
Murmuring sea, and scattered
Sleepy seal upon the shoal.

As breeze is to flesh
And water to earth,
Clinging ice plants
Enliven sheer slate
On precipitous cliffs,
Overspreading all
With orchids on the bluff,
While far below, the benign,
Elegant, cormorant
Parts the sea silently,
Plummeting dinner deep,
With a strong, headlong thrust,
And the will to rise again.

The untended grass, alone,
Starkly craves other water,
But the scaly lizard scratches
Across the matchstick path
In an electric scramble.
Miraculously present,

The Monarch and moth move
Softly with the currents,
As do lazy thoughts that,
Once etched by patient seas,
Create those dark, cool caves
For cerebral refuge
And the essential grace
Of life at beginnings.

•

I am startled
Into wakefulness
After elemental
Absorption.
Seaweed and kelp
Hug the shore
In slippery-thick swirls
And slap a slate cliff base
To race with foam.
The lazy mass
Returns seaward
And plays its way
To surf again.
Past the many arcs
Of ascendant waves,
The sound of crashing.
I hear the crack
Across the back
Of a clam-enclustered rock,
As the swirling sea
Eddies innocently.

The Language of Silence

In the certain silences
When man withdraws
From uncertain dominion
And illusions of power,
He becomes a creature
Vulnerable and real,
True to wonder and
True to the consciousness,
Where unicorns loom large
In imagination's flowery fields.

In elemental harmony,
Nature plays no favorites;
In its outstretched wings
The song of berry and worm
Is borne,
Plucked in timely season
For the upward journey
Into squawking beaks
In nestling down. . .

The flight of silence,
And the dance of silence;
The music of silence
At dawn, at dusk, musky
Twilight and mid-day glare—
The essence of silence—
The rain sounds
On roof and hut,
Mountainside and creek. . .
Snow softness
Oozing into icy grays of slush. . .
Leaf sounds,
And branch sounds;
Ripe pear,
Falling to ground sounds. . .
Windy breeze
And whining wind sounds. . . .

Music moves in silence
Like sandpipers scattering
Footprints
Across the moist sandy shore,
Where, fanning out,
They blossom.
In brief moments,
The frothy sea
Sprawls saltily
Over their tracks,
Licking the granular land
Into sparkling readiness
For the imprint
Of a new moment.

The language of silence
Is lip-read
Music
Vibrating, creating,
Gestating in streams of water
And in streams of air
In the below places
And in the above places
Among mosquito and gnat,
Lice and leech
In teeming cities, seething
With blistering heat, or in
The swarming marsh or wastes—
And still, pendulous flowers
Urge pollination with the
Temptation of a whore's colors
And the scent of a bride
On petal and bough.

Part Eight

She blew
bubbles
In air,
And one
by one
They rose
and burst.
What remains
Is the memory
Of translucence
And spinning
universes
Sailing rainbows
Toward the sun

•

It is dawn,
And I smile.
I know
The shadow
Behind my back
Will be gone
By nightfall,
But
The simplicity
Of it all
Stuns me.

Alarm

I was fast asleep
I thought,
And then a crack
Crashed through dreams
Like a shot.
I sat up,
My ears alert as a dog's,
Listening into the dark night
Heavy with sleep.
Another crack!
An explosion!
What am I subject to
In the violent city?
Whom shall I disturb
Out of dreams?
A neighboring dog barks
And splashes the silence
Of the star-laden night.
Was he dreaming?
Barking at the moon,
Or are prowlers about?
He rests. And then begins
Again. . . . If I call police,
What will they say?
Another insomniac
Confused realities
At 4:00 A.M.?
Ha! Ha, Ha.
I lie down, curling
Into a warm bundle.
What am I responsible for?
Myself. Myself? *Is that right?*
I hope the dark night
Will not stretch its tentacles
Into my room
And the morning news.
My dog is dead.

Boomerang

If I misunderstood
Everything, as you say,
I readily admit
I thought highly of you,
And I must thank you now,
For enlightening me.

Containment

If you are empty,
What have you to give
And what will you accept?
If you are full,
What can you absorb
And what will you discard?

Insubstantiality

You are like moonbeams
Shimmering on the sea:
Reflections of a reflection.
The illusion of luster
Gleams like a perfect jewel,
But does not carry its weight.

For Ruth

Her hair is pulled back
Tightly against her head
In a severe, silvery,
Knotted, no-nonsense
Schoolmarm way,
As if being punished.
Obedient to her will,
Not a strand is in disarray.
She is strong; she is handsome,
She is stringent—
A monolith awaiting heart,
A sepia tint awaiting animation.
Not a smile crosses her face.
Her brows are furrowed,
Her eyes concentrated.
She speaks with precision
And perfect malice,
A master sergeant
At target practice
Hitting the bull's eye
With perfect marksmanship,
And we stay away from her.
She is the wicked stepmother
Of fairy-tale lore,
Everyone an unwanted child
Until we see her art,
Until we see the hidden color,
Until we see the imagination,
Until we see the soaring vision
And the lightness of heart
Hidden under lock and key,
Liberated at last in silence.
You are talented, we say;
You are very gifted, we say
As she tries to smother
The first smile of pleasure—
But we have seen it
And wonder how long
She has waited for praise.

Isolation

He sat in stone-like silence,
Beret and leather jacket,
Impeccably European,
Closely hugging his body.
Perhaps he sheltered the soul
Tempered in history's coil
Or the mind wounded by life
In flight across continents.
I can only conjecture
When towns are savaged,
Children thrust from windows,
And people tormented and torched—
When root, trunk and branch are gone,
When naivete brings ruin,
And horror engulfs the known world,
Refuge in self remains reliably in place.
They say he is a builder,
And that makes great sense to me;
They say he builds far and wide,
And why not? He knows the world;
He has seen its calamitous ruins.
A trio rippled the air,
Tickled the ivory keys,
Thumped the beat of bass,
Sent flurries of flute aloft,
And yet, he did not move.
A dancing child swirled,
Her feet alive on waking
To impromptu abandon,
But he took no notice at all.
The rain; it must be the rain,
Constant, mesmerizing rain,
That drains his energy so
Or lends him the look of a stoic,
I thought, but I was wrong,
For his woman came to feed
The absent one in the self
That was no more.

Hannah

Hannah the sweet;
Hannah the quiet;
Hannah the tender;
Hannah the support;
Hannah the gentle,
Hannah the mother,
Hannah who trusts
Hannah whose face
Speaks of life lived
With grace
Hannah the beautiful
Hannah the lovely
Hannah the ageless
Hannah the guide
Hannah the sage
Hannah who calms
The waters
Hannah my friend.

Lovers

Lovers' farewells need not be sad
When joy of freedom may be had;
A fond chain has power to bind
As surely as the tyrannic kind.
Forego surrender to despair
When someone else is sure to care,
And add not defeat to self promise,
Lest to chains, you'd add a harness.

Chess

We play the game poorly,
But it is a slice of life
And we start out with laughter.
Ha, ha. Who goes first?
Why don't you? No, no,
Let's choose; that's fair.
All right, white or black?
Out go the fists. Okay, choose!
But two pieces are in one hand
And none in the other.
This is a pre-game play,
A comedic act
Destined to go another round.
You go first; it's okay, she insists,
But no, his jaw tightens.
"It has to be fair and square."
At last, it is, and we begin.
Laughter hibernates, postures shift,
And wine awaits the first to move.
The nerves have been readied.

The first foolish moves are made,
Emotions are flushed, lips are pursed.
A competitive glint narrows the eyes,
The kill plainly in view. *Think! Be clever!*
See it! Don't move until you see it!
You know the opponent.
This is no longer a game;
It is his life, and he wants to win.
He will bet anything on it
Now that victory is within grasp.
The air is electric, the room is hot,
We are still and scarcely breathe,
But he makes the wrong move.
Two out of three! Two out of three,
He shouts,
But the hour is late.
There is no chance of that.

The Climb

The tree
Gleams
In the sun
Of my mind's
Light,
Ever, ever
In sight.
"Climb it;
Climb it,"
I say.
"Do it today,"
I plead.
"Your feet
are sure,
Your arms
Are strong.
What can go
Wrong?"

The bark
Is silent,
And each branch
The same,
But the topmost
Leaves
            care.
"Please, oh please,"
They cry.
"Touch me. Touch me,
            Or I die."
"Oh rustling leaves,
I hear your call,
But I am a man
Afraid to fall."
            "Do not pass me by;
I have waited for you,"
They howled.

"Oh glum leaf,
Do not cry.
You wrench me so!"
Loathe to stay,
And loathe to go,
You sigh
"Ah reluctant me,
What is this destiny?"
How sad you are,
But the height
Seems shorter
As step by
Cautious step
You find your way.
"Oh god," you pray,
"Make it easy.
I have not been
This far before."

The day is hot
On exertion's face
But the clambering
Changes not its pace.
Rainbow dew now
Beads your brow,
And shafts
Of streaming rays
Filter the way.
"Oh what a fool
I have been," you shout,
This is ecstasy!"
I bellow
            from below:
"Are you at the very top?"
"Heck no," I hear from afar.
"I have been touched by sea mist,
And seen cormorant at play."

The Promise

Gusts of wind whipped
Through the trees
And rattled the old leaves
Burnished in gold.
Aflame with amber
And tarnished copper,
They swirled
Through deserted streets
In excited flurries,
And there they rested
In weary clumps
Of earthy browns
At the first hard rains.
The soggy protest
Of humiliation
At so forlorn a state
Had come to an end
After a vibrant
And proud summer
Of lush foliage,
But the shamefaced trees
Trembled in exposed limbs
And vowed to address
Their nakedness anew.
It was a promise
They meant to keep.

Imperatives for a Life of Reason
In a Place Where Nature Refuses to Die

Summer heat, fields of daisies
And raccoons of the night,
I address you.
Poppy-strewn dunes, succulents,
Sea breeze and wet-kissing fog,
I address you, too.
Old rock, pocked by howling winds
That whip through the night where
Sea otters make their home,
You know how I feel.
Grazing cows, black bull beauty,
And hoof-hewn, grass-strewn paths
Moist with morning dew in Monterey,
You too know how I feel.
Roan stallion and silver mare,
Grazing by the gleaming ocean,
What would I not dare for a share
Of those deep blue-green blades,
Velvet plush, frosty sage and clover?
Do you not know I love your pregnant
Furrows of artichoke hearts?

The Canopy

The canopy
I stand under
Is very strong
And has no posts.
It is a shield
Without armor;
It is a house.
I live in it;
It is a home
All may enter.
It has no doors.

Soft Touch

You are before me,
You are at my side,
You are within.
We cannot touch,
But I reach you.
Like a whisper in the wind,
The sound soothes your brow
And I hear you sigh.

Joy

Joy never dies.
It is a balm
That lingers
In memory.
Do not believe
The false one's cry
That dissuades you
Otherwise.
You have been touched,
And cannot have
What cannot be
More than all.
Did you not know
It was a gift?